of 2014

Preserving Access
to California
Higher Education

George S. Park
Robert J. Lempert

RAND Education

RAND

California's ability to preserve the current levels of access to its system of public higher education is being threatened by increasing enrollments, pressures on the state budget, and the increasing costs of higher education. This study addressed the conditions under which California can preserve access over the next two decades. In addressing these conditions, the study used a new approach to decision making under uncertainty, called exploratory modeling, that combines traditional quantitative forecasting techniques with insights from scenario planning.

This effort was one element of a larger program performed by RAND Education to study issues of direct relevance to California's higher education system. As such, this work should be of interest to California policymakers dealing with higher education within the state, as well as to policymakers in other states who may be facing issues similar to those confronting California.

This program was supported by the California Education Round Table, which includes leaders from the California Community College, California State University, and University of California systems, as well as from California private universities. This work benefitted greatly from the direction and data obtained from these representatives, as well as from the California Postsecondary Education Commission.

CONTENTS

FIGURES

TABLES

For over 35 years, California's policy of providing a college education to all citizens who could benefit from it has enabled California to lead the nation in making public higher education available and has helped the state generate great wealth and social mobility. Now, in the emerging information economy, this provision of widespread higher education is more important than ever.

Several trends, however, suggest that California's ability to maintain, much less increase, high levels of college education may be at risk. First, with the state's growing population, many more students will seek access to higher education. This "Tidal Wave II" could present California public colleges and universities with a million or more additional students. Second, the fraction of state resources devoted to higher education has been dropping in recent years because of growing demands on the state budget that compete with education, such as corrections, health, and welfare. Without a significant change in priorities, it is likely that funding for higher education will continue to be limited. Third, the costs of higher education have been rising faster than inflation over the past 35 years. While many sectors of the economy have slowed rising output costs through significant productivity improvements, the higher education sector has not shown comparable improvements in productivity.

The challenge for policymakers is to assure access to California higher education in the face of these trends. The problem is complicated by the fact that each of these trends is uncertain. No one knows precisely how many students will seek access to higher education, nor what funds will be available from the state, nor which productivity improvements are possible or desirable in higher education. A number of studies have assessed these trends and recommended actions state policymakers should take. These studies take the traditional approach of basing their recommendations on a single best estimate of each of these trends, essentially ignoring much of the uncertainty that exists about the future.

When uncertainties are large, however, projections of the future are often wrong. Policies based on best estimates can fail if the future turns out differently than expected. In addition, decision makers can spend too much time debating the most likely future rather than developing flexible, robust strategies that can take advantage of fortuitous opportunities and avoid unexpected difficulties.

Our study, conducted in 1997, used a new approach to make a quantitative assessment of the various trends facing California higher education and to suggest the implications they have for current policy choices. This approach combines two previously distinct strands of strategic planning methodology. The traditional forecasting techniques employed in most studies of California higher education use sophisticated models and available data to project likely trends. These approaches provide much rigor but have difficulty coping with the uncertainty inherent in most decisions. Recently, many public and private sector organizations have begun to use scenario planning techniques that help decision makers bring uncertainty into their planning and help different stakeholders agree on a framework for discussion. However, scenario planning as currently practiced cannot make use of available quantitative information.

Our new approach, called *exploratory modeling,* exploits new computer capabilities to combine quantitative forecasting with scenario planning. Using this approach, we examined how the interrelationship of three key factors—demand for higher education, competition for state revenues, and potential productivity improvements—may affect the future of California higher education. We used computer simulation models and data similar to those used by other studies. Rather than projecting the most likely trends, however, we examined a large number of plausible scenarios for the future. We made visual representations of these scenarios and then used these "landscapes of plausible futures" to clarify key uncertainties facing decision makers, to provide a framework that can be used by the different stakeholders to debate differing views of the future, and to compare the effects of different policy choices.

While it may seem that abandoning a best estimate for a large set of plausible futures complicates the decision-making problem, it actually provides real and very useful information. Perhaps surprisingly, when we trade the question "What is most likely to happen in the future?" for "Which policy choice deals best with the uncertainty we face?" the complexity posed by an unpredictable future often falls away and reveals a small set of clear choices.

This report focuses on the first step in an exploratory modeling analysis: creating landscapes of plausible futures for California higher education and using these landscapes to identify the uncertainties and trends most salient to decision makers' choices. In a subsequent effort, we hope to compare the performance of a large number of potential policy choices against these landscapes to help policymakers choose the best policy.

Our study shows that trends in two key areas dominate the question of future access to California higher education: future state funding and feasible improvements in productivity. We found that

- If the fraction of the state general fund allocated to higher education remains close to current levels (breaking a 20-year downward trend) and if productivity increases at faster than historic rates, California will avoid serious access deficits. If either of these fails to occur, however, California could face large access deficits.

- If the fraction of the state general fund allocated to higher education continues to fall, California can maintain access only by increasing fees well beyond any amount now envisioned in the political debate or by achieving productivity increases that are very large relative to historical rates of improvement. At present, it is not known whether such productivity improvements are possible and, if they are, how to achieve them.

- The above conclusions are largely insensitive to any plausible trends in future demand for higher education.

The uncertainties related to the future of California higher education are real and are a fundamental part of the challenge facing policymakers. Large uncertainties are not, however, a barrier to effective decision making. This study suggests that a flexible, robust strategy for ensuring future access to California higher education must pay close attention to three critical questions: Can the state readjust its financial commitments in order to maintain current funding levels for higher education? Can the higher education system improve its productivity significantly faster than it has over the past 35 years? and Can a public higher education system with high fees and high aid successfully serve a broad spectrum of California's diverse population?

ACKNOWLEDGMENTS

This study would not have been possible without the generous cooperation of the California Education Round Table and its Technical Advisory Committee, whose members include the chancellors and other leaders of the California Community College, California State University, and University of California systems. They made their data available to us and provided thoughtful comments and advice throughout our work. We also benefited greatly from the help of current and former RAND colleagues, especially Roger Benjamin, Steve Carroll, Bill Lewis, Michael Shires, Dominic Brewer, Susan Gates, and Ann Stone. Our reviewers, in particular Emmett Keeler, did much to help us improve our work. The contents are of course our responsibility, but our editor, Jeri O'Donnell, did an excellent job helping make our prose more precise.

Chapter One

INTRODUCTION

Over the past 35 years, the state of California has built an impressive program of higher education. Anchored by its three-tiered public system, higher education has made immense contributions to the state's economy and the widespread opportunity (however imperfect) that has characterized California society. The state's commitment to higher education was codified in the 1960 Master Plan, which guaranteed that all individuals who could benefit from a college education would receive one. But whatever higher education has contributed to California in the past, it is likely to be even more important in the future. In our evolving information economy, a college degree is one of the key determinants of economic success. California's economy may become significantly poorer if the workforce does not become increasingly college educated. In addition, the state's social cohesion may suffer if restricted access to higher education widens income disparities among different ethnic groups in the state's population.

TRENDS AFFECTING HIGHER EDUCATION

Several decades-long trends suggest that California's ability to maintain, much less increase, high levels of college education may be in danger:

- Demand for higher education, which has grown sevenfold in California since World War II, is expected to continue growing over the next two decades as the current bulge of a million or more students in the elementary schools works its way through the system. This so-called Tidal Wave II could be smaller or

1

larger depending on whether the children of groups with traditionally low levels of education, particularly recent Hispanic immigrants, attend college at rates approaching those of whites and Asians.

- The percentage of the state budget that supports higher education has declined over the past 20 years as state spending on health, welfare, and corrections has increased dramatically. Public resistance to increased taxes has largely capped total state spending. Thus, state resources per student in higher education have declined and, without a significant change in state spending priorities, may continue to do so into the future. Concurrently, federal funding for student loans and financial aid has grown slowly over recent years and may continue to do so given pressures on the federal budget.

- The costs of higher education have risen consistently faster than inflation over the past 35 years. For instance, the Higher Education Price Index (HEPI), which measures the real increase in the prices of the goods and services used by higher education institutions, has outpaced the Consumer Price Index (CPI) by an annual average of one full percentage point. In other sectors of the economy, such sustained imbalances in the cost of inputs have led to either large changes in productivity, often accompanied by large organizational changes, or decline.

There is wide agreement about these basic trends, but there is a broad spectrum of opinion as to how deleterious they will be for the future of California higher education. For instance, the Research and Planning Department at the University of California predicts that state funding for higher education will show healthy growth over the next two decades, as the state economy grows and the fraction of state funding that goes to higher education remains constant (Copperud and Geiser, 1996). Conversely, Shires (1996) of the California Public Policy Institute of California predicts state support for higher education will drop precipitously as increased state spending on corrections cuts the fraction of the state general fund allocated to higher education in half. Similarly, there are many different projections of the precise number of students who will seek access to higher education.

TRADITIONAL ANALYTIC APPROACH

In the traditional approach, a policy study would assess each of these conflicting predictions and decide which are the most likely. Based on this "best estimate" of the future, the study would then recommend the policies most likely to succeed. This traditional approach sometimes works very well, but policies based on one best estimate can fail if another future comes to pass. Unfortunately, decision makers and policy analysts, like most people, have a strong tendency to underestimate their uncertainty about the future.[1] They focus on some single best estimate, often the one they think most likely or most supportive of the case they wish to make.

The dangers for California higher education are clear. Policies predicated on high levels of state funding that never materialize or on overambitious estimates of productivity improvements could deny large numbers of potential students a higher education. However, policies predicated on overly pessimistic assumptions could waste resources and disrupt lives, overfixing institutions that are not broken. In addition, decision makers can spend too much time debating the most likely future rather than developing flexible, robust strategies that can take advantage of fortuitous opportunities and avoid unexpected difficulties.

We believe that the differing predictions of the trends facing California higher education represent real uncertainty about the future that is difficult if not impossible to resolve. In some cases—such as the sensitivity of student demand to changes in tuition—there currently is not enough information to predict well. In other cases—such as the budget priorities of future legislatures and the impact of information technology on the classroom—the phenomena involved are inherently unpredictable. Thus, the different predictions for the future of California higher education do not reflect faulty analysis by one party or another so much as the fact that such factors as future funding and demand for education result from an inherently unpredictable set of future political and individual decisions.

---

[1]See, for instance, Chapter 6, "Human Judgment about and with Uncertainty," in Morgan and Henrion, 1990.

NEW ANALYTIC APPROACH

Our study used a new approach to make a quantitative assessment of the various trends facing California higher education and to suggest the implications they have for current policy choices. Rather than projecting the most likely trends, we examined a large number of plausible scenarios for the future. We made visual representations of these scenarios and used these "landscapes of plausible futures" to clarify the key uncertainties facing decision makers, to provide a framework that different stakeholders can use to debate differing views of the future, and to compare the effects of different policy choices.

Our approach combines two previously distinct strands of strategic planning methodology. Traditional forecasting employs sophisticated models and available quantitative data to project likely trends. This type of approach provides much rigor but has difficulty coping with the uncertainty inherent in most decisions. Recently, many public and private sector organizations have begun to use scenario planning techniques, such as those developed by Royal Dutch Shell and the Global Business Network.[2] These approaches help decision makers bring uncertainty into their planning and help different stakeholders agree on a framework for discussion. However, scenario planning as currently practiced cannot make use of available quantitative information.

Our new approach, called *exploratory modeling* (Bankes, 1993, 1994), combines quantitative forecasts with scenario planning. We exploit the new capabilities provided by wedding information technology (primarily networked computer workstations and powerful desktop graphics) to new concepts of decision making under extreme uncertainty.[3] In this study, we used computer models to describe future

---

[2]Wack (1985) describes Royal Dutch Shell's developments in scenario planning. Schwartz (1991) provides one of the classic descriptions of scenario planning methodologies; his Global Business Network can be found at www.gbn.org. Dewar, et al. (1993) describe assumption-based planning, the RAND-developed version of these methods.

[3]The field of decision analysis largely deals with uncertainty about the future that can be characterized by well-known probability distributions. Exploratory modeling can address cases of extreme uncertainty for which the probability distributions are un-

enrollments in the three public California systems of higher education—University of California (UC), California State University
(CSU), and the community colleges (CCs); the revenues available for
undergraduate education; the effects of potential productivity improvements; and the impact of potential fee increases. The quantitative data and mathematical representations we used are similar to
and in many instances identical to those used by other analysts. But
rather than use these models to make best-estimate projections, we
used them as constraints on the range of plausible futures for
California higher education.

One reason our approach is useful is that there is often a great deal of
information about a problem that, although insufficient for making
accurate predictions, is nonetheless useful for making decisions. For
instance, simple accounting relationships among the flows of students and money through the higher education system impose important constraints on the future. While it may seem that abandoning a best estimate for a large set of plausible futures complicates the
decision-making problem, the large set of plausible scenarios represents real and very useful information. Perhaps surprisingly, when
we trade the question "What is most likely to happen in the future?"
for "Which policy choice deals best with the uncertainty we face?"
the complexity posed by an unpredictable future often falls away and
reveals a small set of clear choices.[4]

This report focuses on the first step in an exploratory modeling analysis: creating landscapes of plausible futures for California higher
education and using these landscapes to identify those uncertainties
and trends most salient to decision makers' choices. In the future,
we hope to address the second step: comparing the performance of
a large number of potential policy choices against these landscapes
to help policymakers choose the best policy consistent with their risk
profile and their own expectations about the future.

---

known. Some concepts similar to exploratory modeling can be found in the policy
region analysis of Watson and Buede (1987).

[4]See, for instance, Lempert, Schlesinger, and Bankes, 1996, which uses exploratory
modeling to show that an adaptive strategy dominates the other policy options
currently proposed to address the problem of global climate change.

ORGANIZATION OF THIS REPORT

The next chapter of this report summarizes the data and models we used to describe the California higher education system. Chapter 3 presents our landscapes of plausible futures for California higher education; Chapter 4 presents our conclusions. Five appendices describe the details of our calculations and provide additional results to support the arguments laid out in the main body of this report.

Chapter Two

ANALYTIC FRAMEWORK

This chapter describes the models and data used in our analysis. The discussion is organized around four general factors that affect the future of California higher education (see Figure 1). The first of these, **exogenous trends**, are factors over which policymakers, in this case the members of the California Round Table, have little or no control. The second type, **policy levers**, are factors controlled by policymakers. The third type, **measures**, are ways in which to assess whether the performance of the higher education system is good or bad. **Relationships**, fourth, are the ways in which the measures are related to changes in the levers and exogenous factors.

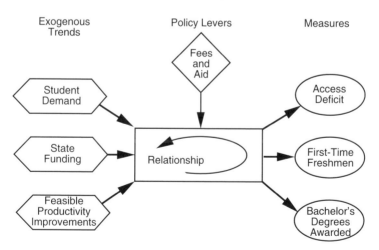

Figure 1—Key Factors Considered in Our Analysis

Our study focused on three of the key exogenous factors affecting California higher education: (1) increasing demand for higher education due to a growing population and increases in participation rates among traditionally underrepresented demographic groups, (2) potentially constrained state funding for higher education, and (3) the degree to which productivity improvements can feasibly offset rising costs for higher education and decreasing revenues. These factors are shown as hexagons in Figure 1.

We chose a range of estimates for each of these factors, constrained by the available information. This information includes past trends and future constraints such as demographic projections and limits on the state budget. We chose the ranges in the context of the conclusions of the study. For instance, we chose an especially wide range of estimates for future demand because we argue that this factor is relatively unimportant, and we chose a narrow range for future changes in productivity because we argue that this factor may be crucial to the future of California higher education.

We considered three simple measures of the performance of the higher education system. Shown as ovals in Figure 1, these are

- Access deficit: the number of individuals who wish to enroll but cannot be accommodated. This is a clear and widely used measure that refers directly to one of the goals of the Master Plan. As discussed in detail below, the access deficit is an estimate of the number of individuals who wish to attend a California institution of higher learning but either are turned away because the institution has insufficient financial resources or are deterred from enrolling because of fee increases.

- Number of first-time freshmen: a useful measure when time to graduation varies, since lingering upperclassmen can increase enrollments while reducing an institution's ability to admit new students.

- Bachelor's degrees awarded: a rough measure of an output of the higher education system that has some importance for society, recognizing that California higher education also provides training, performs research, and contributes to society in a variety of other ways. Degrees awarded is also a measure in which California is currently weak. California ranks 16th among the states in total college enrollment per capita, but 46th in degrees awarded per capita.

We concentrated on one policy lever, student fees, the focus of significant debate in recent years. The division between exogenous factors and levers is to some extent a choice of the decision maker. For instance, the Round Table has some influence over the proportion of state funds allocated to higher education. It could choose to take actions that might expand this influence. Similarly, the Round Table could take actions to affect the feasible levels of productivity improvement in the higher education system. The choice of levers and exogenous factors in this study is meant as an initial examination of the range of policy options. In future work, we hope to expand our consideration to different policy levers, particularly those associated with improving productivity.

We considered a variety of relationships that determine how the exogenous trends and policy levers affect the measures. We focused on the flow of students and money through each of California's three public systems of higher education—UC, CSU, and the CCs. In brief, students wish to attend a public college or university. This demand is influenced by the level of fees. Each system determines how many students it will admit, based in part on its capacity as measured by the revenues available per student and by how efficiency improvements affect the revenues required per student. Each system gains revenues from state funds (CCs also get local funds) and from fees paid by enrolled students. Graduation and advancement rates affect the number of degrees awarded and the size of the student population. The student population, in turn, affects the revenues each system gains from fees, the total revenues per student, and the access deficit. In our analysis, we considered coupled flows among all three public California systems.

There are, of course, relationships that are not considered here. For instance, we did not consider the effect increased fees may have on speeding the rate at which students advance through the system. Nor did we consider the effects of other major uncertainties, such as changes in affirmative action policies or changes in immigration or citizenship rules that might affect the number of people considered eligible to enroll in California public colleges and universities. Nonetheless, the relationships we considered provide a solid basis for understanding the impacts of and interactions among the trends affecting California higher education.

The remainder of this chapter provides an overview of our analytic framework. Full mathematical details can be found in the appendices.

TRENDS IN STUDENT DEMAND

The first key trend facing California higher education is an increasing number of potential students. Most observers expect that the demand for access to California higher education over the next 20 years will surge, though there is disagreement over how many individuals actually will and should seek to be accommodated. In our analysis, we considered four alternative estimates of the demand for higher education in California. Together they span the plausible range of assumptions about the size of what is often called Tidal Wave II.

Our estimates of future demand are based on projections of California's population and use of the "participation rate" methodology of Shires (1996). Following Shires, we assumed that the demand for higher education is equal to what the enrollment would be in the absence of financial constraints. We estimated these unconstrained enrollments in two steps, as more fully described in Appendix A. First, we used data on past higher education enrollments and California demographics to calculate the average rate at which individuals from different ethnic, age, and gender cohorts participate in the UC, CSU, and CC systems. Second, we multiplied demographic projections for the future size of each cohort by these participation rates to estimate enrollments through 2014. As in Shires's work, we tracked the number of students in each class (freshman, sophomore, junior, and senior) and the transfers between the systems. We augmented Shires's model to include advancement and graduation rates, which we used to estimate the number of seniors awarded bachelor's degrees each year by UC and CSU.

Figure 2 shows our four alternative enrollment estimates. For each estimate, we calculated the number of students enrolled in the UC, CSU, and CC systems each year from 1996 through 2014. Each estimate uses a different set of assumptions about participation rates,

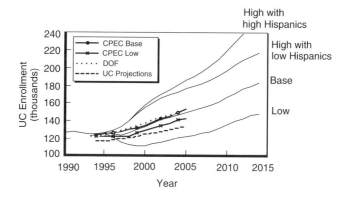

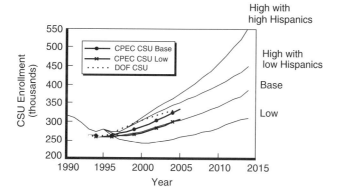

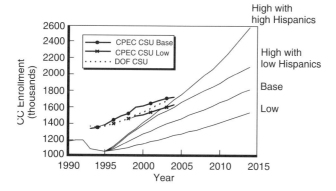

**Figure 2—Alternative Enrollment Estimates Compared to Projections from
· Other Studies**

but they all use common projections of California's future demo-graphics. The line labeled "base" in each frame of Figure 2 shows our enrollment estimates for each system using the participation rates derived from enrollment data provided by the California Postsecondary Education Commission (CPEC, 1995b) and the California State Demographic Unit's data (1995) for 1993 through 1995. For the high and low demand estimates, we used participation rates 20% higher and 20% lower, respectively, than those used for our base estimates. For the highest demand estimate, we started with participation rates 20% higher than the base values for each cohort and then further increased the participation rates for the Hispanic cohort by 4% annually. Currently, Hispanics represent the state's fastest growing population group and have college participation rates significantly lower than do other groups. The highest demand estimate represents a case in which Hispanics are attending college with a participation rate increasing annually by 4%, chosen so that their participation rate in the UC system at the end of 20 years is nearly equal to that of non-Hispanic whites.[1]

Figure 2 also compares our four alternative enrollment estimates to projections made by CPEC (1995b), and to the State Department of Finance ("DOF" in the figure) and the University of California (University of California, 1996). While the methodologies used to gener-ate these other projections differ from our model in how they handle factors such as student flow, admissions assumptions, and defini-tions of student status, they are all based on state demographics in terms of either total population of cohorts or high school graduates of cohorts, which is proportional to first order. The differences be-tween the lines in the CC (lower) plot in Figure 2 arise from differ-ences in the way students are counted; in fact, our numbers agree closely with CPEC's Student Profiles reported data for the CCs from 1989 to 1994.[2] For the period 1995 to 2005, for which enrollment

---

[1]For each alternative enrollment estimate, we report the number of students in each system, since the data used to calculate the coefficients for Eqs. A4 and A5 (see Ap-pendix A) are reported as 'headcounts.' To translate our enrollment estimates into aggregated full-year full-time equivalents (FTEs), multiply the reported values by 0.96 for the UC system, 0.75 for CSU, and 0.64 for the CCs. Unless noted otherwise, en-rollments are given in headcount numbers throughout this report.

[2] See "Student Profiles, 1995," CPEC, October 1995, pp. 1–11 (www.cpec.ca.gov/stuprfl/stuprfl.html).

projections are available from all sources shown here, our baseline enrollment estimate is in general agreement with the other projections. Other studies have made different choices—for instance, estimating participation rates using 1989 enrollment and demographics data.[3]

The alternative enrollment estimates we used in this study span the breadth of plausible demand projections generally put forth for the future of California higher education. As shown in Table 1, the range of estimates spans over a million students (the projected size of Tidal Wave II) and is significantly larger than the range of estimates usually discussed in the debate on California higher education. We chose this large range in order to support the argument in the next chapter that uncertainties about future demand are not one of the key factors affecting the future of California higher education.

Table 1

Estimates of Future Demand for Higher Education

Estimate	Description in Model	Result in 2014
High, with high Hispanic participation	Participation rates 1.2 times larger than basecase. Hispanic participation rates grow an additional 4% annually.	3.2 million students in California higher education, 2.5 times 1995 enrollment. Hispanics participate at same rate as whites and Asians.
High, with low Hispanic participation	Participation rates 1.2 times larger than basecase.	2.8 million students in California higher education. Hispanics attend at current low rate compared to whites and Asians.
Base	Basecase participation rates.	2.4 million students in California higher education.
Low	Participation rates 0.8 times smaller than basecase.	2 million students in California higher education, 1.5 times 1995 enrollment.

---

[3]See, for instance, Shires, 1996.

TRENDS IN STATE FUNDING

Besides demographic trends, a second key issue facing California higher education is the financial support that will be available from the state government. UC, CSU, and the CCs draw their income from a variety of sources, but revenues from the state general fund constitute a substantial fraction of each system's funds for undergraduate education. (CCs are additionally supported by local property taxes.) From 1970 to 1996, the fraction of the general fund allocated to higher education dropped from 17% to 12% as state spending on other priorities—particularly corrections, health, and welfare—increased. There is much disagreement as to whether this decline in state higher education funding will continue into the future. In our analysis, we considered five alternative estimates of state general fund allocations to higher education as a way to span the plausible range of assumptions about future funds.

Our estimates of future revenues are based on data describing the current sources of revenues. It is not a straightforward task to determine the funds allocated to undergraduate education in each system: each receives funds from a variety of sources, and many types of spending benefit several missions within a system. For instance, UC building maintenance benefits both undergraduate and graduate education. We thus made the simplifying assumption that funds available for undergraduate education in each system come from three sources—the state general fund, student fees, and, for the CCs, property taxes. We estimated the current total general fund and property tax allocations to undergraduate higher education by multiplying CPEC data on 1995 spending per undergraduate in each system—$6,809 for UC, $4,734 for CSU, and $3,050 for the CCs (about equally divided between local property taxes and the state)—by CPEC's 1995 enrollment data (CPEC, 1995a,b). We estimated the current average fees per student in each system from CPEC data on total enrollment and the total revenues from fees. As described in detail in Appendix B, we then projected future general fund and property tax allocations to higher education by assuming they grow at some annual rate. We estimated future revenues from fees in each system by multiplying future fees by our estimates of the number of enrolled students. Fees can, of course, affect the number of enrolled students, as we discuss below. In this analysis, we focused only on revenues associated with the costs of current operations. We leave the important topic of capital costs for future work.

We made five alternative estimates of future allocations by the state general fund to undergraduate education, as shown in Figure 3. All five assume that the California economy, and thus the state general fund, grow at 2.7% annually.[4] For our "optimistic" funding estimate, we assumed, as does the UC Research and Planning Department (Copperud and Geiser, 1996), that the fraction of the general fund allocated to higher education remains constant at its current level, and thus that the general fund revenues allocated to each of the three systems grow at 2.7% per year. For our two "pessimistic" estimates, we assumed that the share of the general fund going to higher education rapidly declines because of increased spending on corrections, K–12 education, and other programs (Shires, 1996;

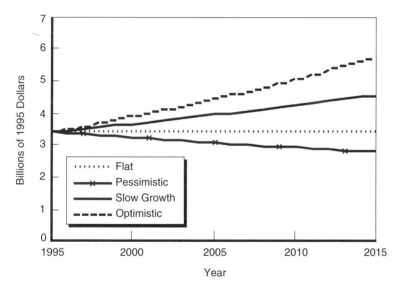

Figure 3—Alternative Estimates of State General Fund Allocations to Higher Education

---

[4]This is the growth rate projected by UCLA for the California economy from 1996 to 2005. We extended this projection to 2014.

Carroll, et al., 1995), so that the net general fund revenues allocated to the three systems decline. For one of these estimates, "pessimistic, without 98," we assumed that state revenues to all three systems decline at –1% annually. For the other pessimistic estimate, "pessimistic, with 98," we assumed that the CC share of these declining revenues increases because of Proposition 98 mandates, so state revenues to the CCs grow at 1.5% annually while state revenues to UC and CSU decline at –3.5% annually. (Note that the two pessimistic estimates have the same total dollars allocated to higher education, so only four distinct estimates are seen in Figure 3.) We also included two intermediate estimates, "slow growth" and "flat," which have general fund allocations to each of the three systems growing, respectively, at 1.5% and 0% annually. For each of our alternative estimates, we assumed that property tax revenues to the CCs grow at 3% per year (Shires, 1996). Note that we did not consider potential changes in federal funding that might affect UC, nor did we consider property tax revenues that might affect the CCs. We left these important topics to future work.

We summarize this range of estimates for future state funding in Table 2. Note that total state funding varies by $3 billion, which is roughly the same total amount California spends today on higher education. This large range reflects the fact that the total size of the state budget, measured as a proportion of the state economy, is currently fixed by the state constitution, and that large segments of the budget are currently growing at a rate that, if continued, will largely squeeze out the state funds available for higher education.

EFFECT OF FUNDING ON ACCESS

The state funding available for higher education may strongly influence the number of individuals able to obtain a college education. Our earlier estimates of future demand were based on enrollment projections in the absence of financial strictures. Now we present our estimate of enrollments under conditions of financial constraints and introduce the concept of an access deficit. We have followed Shires (1996) in defining the access deficit as the difference between the projected, unconstrained demand for higher education assuming fees stay at their current level, and the number of students who could

Table 2

Estimates of Future State Funding of Higher Education

Estimate	Description in Model	Result in 2014
Optimistic	Fraction of state general fund allotted to higher education remains constant.	Higher education receives $5.8 billion, about 12% of state general fund, reversing 20-year trend (1976–1997). Growth rates of state spending on health and welfare, corrections, and/or K–12 decrease significantly, or taxes increase significantly.
Slow growth	State funds allotted to higher education increase 1.5% annually.	Higher education receives $4.6 billion from state general fund.
Flat	State funds allotted to higher education remain constant.	Higher education receives $3.4 billion from state general fund.
Pessimistic, without 98	State funds to each sector of higher education decrease 1% annually.	Higher education receives $2.8 billion, about 6% of state general fund and 80% of 1995 levels, continuing 20-year downward trend.
Pessimistic, with 98	State funds to higher education decrease 1% annually. Funds to CCs increase consistent with Proposition 98.	Same as 'pessimistic, without 98,' but funds to UC and CSU drop to nearly 50% of 1995 levels while funds to CCs increase by 30% over 1995 levels.

be accommodated at some projected level of future state funding with some future level of fees

Shires argues that prior to the recession of the early 1990s, funding for California higher education was largely demand driven—the state provided funding to serve projected enrollments. Since the recession, however, funding has been budget driven—the state allocates the funds it can afford to spend on higher education, and each of the systems does what it can with that allocation. Following Shires, we estimated enrollments in each of our scenarios using two simple rules for admissions: (1) unconstrained admissions, in which students are allowed to continue to attend each system at the same rates they have in the past, and (2) constrained admissions, in which enrollment may be limited so that the level of spending per undergraduate remains constant in real terms. The unconstrained admissions rule gives demand-driven enrollment estimates; the constrained admissions rule produces budget-driven enrollment estimates. We thus calculated the access deficit for any particular scenario, as described in detail in Appendix E, as the difference between enrollments estimated using the unconstrained rules with no fee increase and enrollments estimated using constrained admission rules.

Figure 4 shows the UC and CSU access deficits for the pessimistic and optimistic estimates of future state funding with no fee increases. Note that for both systems, the access deficit is small to nonexistent for the optimistic levels of funding but large for the pessimistic levels.

TRENDS IN PRODUCTIVITY

Improvements in productivity are the third key factor affecting California higher education. Productivity is a difficult topic for a number for reasons. In recent years, many private sector organizations have significantly improved their productivity and thereby reduced their costs. Such improvements should also be possible in the public sector, and, indeed, many public sector institutions have made progress with them in recent years. Nonetheless, productivity is often more difficult to measure and improve in the public sector compared to the private sector, since the goals of the typical public sector institution and the interests of its stakeholders are more diverse than is the case for most private sector organizations. For instance, there is a danger that attempts to improve productivity in public institutions of higher education could focus only on reducing an institution's quantifiable costs, damaging some of the institution's other critical yet more intangible characteristics, such as the quality of its education.

There were not enough available data and analyses to enable us to estimate the rate of productivity improvement possible in California higher education or to recommend steps the Round Table should take to improve productivity. Instead, we explored a large range of

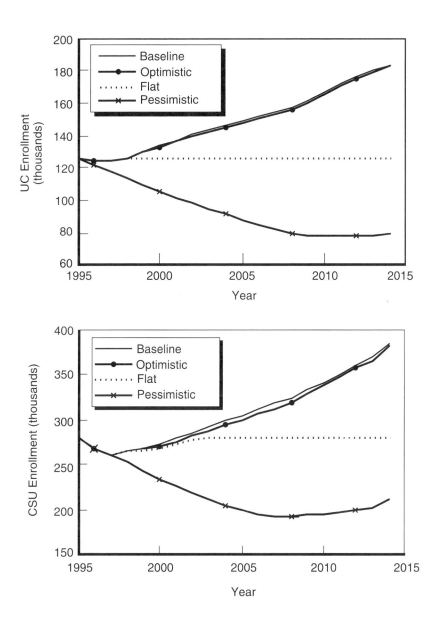

Figure 4—Effect of Alternative Estimates of State General Fund on UC and CSU Access Deficit

assumptions about the feasible rate of productivity improvements within California higher education and examined the consequences of these assumptions. We show that assumptions about feasible productivity improvements, along with assumptions about future state funding, are the key factors affecting the future of California higher education.

In his work on productivity in public sector institutions, Epstein (1992) describes two types of productivity improvements: efficiency and effectiveness. Efficiency refers to the level and quality of service an organization can produce from a given amount of input resources. Effectiveness refers to the extent to which an organization meets the needs of its stakeholders and customers. Epstein provides two specific ways to demonstrate productivity improvements. First, an organization can demonstrate a measurable reduction in cost while maintaining or improving key measures of effectiveness. Second, an organization can demonstrate a measurable improvement in one or more key effectiveness indicators without increasing input costs. We considered both of these forms of productivity improvements in our analysis.

We took graduation and advancement rates as our (admittedly crude) measures of effectiveness for UC, CSU, and the CCs. Graduation rates are directly related to the number of bachelor's degrees awarded, an important factor for both the individual students and the society at large; and advancement rates are directly related to average time to graduation, an important indicator used by UC and CSU to assess their performance. As described in detail in Appendix A, our model uses graduation rates to estimate the number of degrees awarded from our estimates of the number of seniors, and it uses advancement rates to estimate the number of members of one class who move on to the next. For our measure of efficiency, we took the minimum revenues required per student in each system. As described in detail in Appendices B, D, and E, we used this value to determine the maximum enrollment, and thus access deficits, in each system under conditions of financial constraints.

We considered five alternative assumptions about the feasible rate of efficiency improvement in California higher education: –2%, –1%, 0%, 1%, and 2% annually. Figure 5 shows UC and CSU enrollments

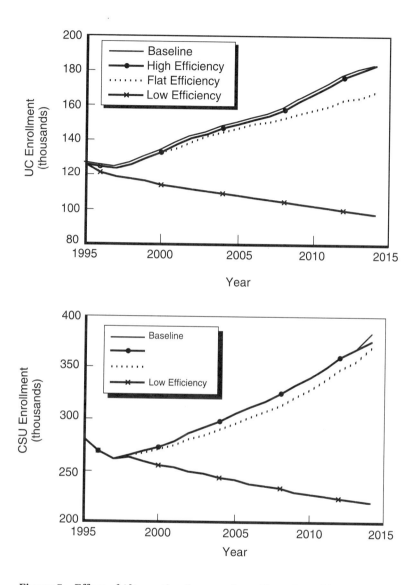

Figure 5—Effect of Alternative Assumptions About Feasible Efficiency
Improvements on UC and CSU Enrollment

for the high, low, and middle values in this range. In each of these cases, we held effectiveness, as measured by graduation and advancement rates, constant. What is evident is that a high rate of efficiency growth reduces the access deficit almost to zero, while a negative rate of growth causes very large access deficits, similar to those caused by the pessimistic estimate of revenues from the state general fund (see Figure 3).

We took our plausible range of efficiency improvements from data on the costs of inputs to higher education over the last 35 years. The Higher Education Price Index (HEPI) measures the real increase in the price of the services and goods, such as salaries and equipment, that U.S. higher education institutions use in their operations. Figure 6 shows that the price of these inputs has consistently outpaced inflation in the rest of the economy, as measured by the Consumer Price Index (CPI), by up to 3% per year. On average, prices to higher education have risen 1% faster than inflation over the last 15 years. The figures shown here are nationwide averages; independent data do not exist for California institutions. Our choice of the range of annual efficiency improvements shown in Figure 5 is somewhat narrower than the range of variation in input prices shown in Figure 6. This conservative range of estimates, summarized in Table 3, should strengthen our claims that the actual, though currently unknown, level of feasible efficiency improvements will be one of the key factors determining the future of California higher education.

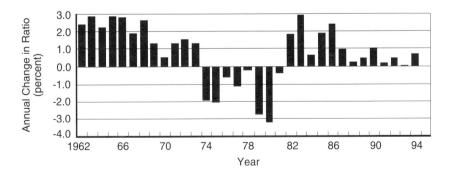

Figure 6—Cost of Inputs to Higher Education, 1962–95

Table 3

Estimates of Future Changes in Productivity

Estimate	Description in Model	Result in 2014
Efficiency	Changes in efficiency, as defined in Eq. D1 (Appendix D), range from -2% to 2% per year.	At -2% annual change, institutions would need 50% more dollars per student than in 1995.
		At 2% annual change, institutions would provide same quality education for 30% fewer dollars per student than in 1995.
Effectiveness	Changes in effectiveness, as defined in Eq. D2, range from -0.5% to 1.5% per year.	Virtually all students would graduate in 4 years if effectiveness improved at 1.5% per year.

We also considered five estimates of the rate of improvement in effectiveness (advancement and graduation rates): –0.5%, 0%, 0.5%, 1.0%, and 1.5%. As with efficiency, few data and analyses are available for estimating what improvements are possible. Thus, we based our range of effectiveness improvement on comparisons of the number of bachelor's degrees awarded per enrolled student in different states. As Table 3 shows, we chose a high estimate (1.5%) of annual effectiveness improvement as the rate necessary to achieve a four-year time to degree for nearly all UC cohorts and for a majority of CSU cohorts. Figure 7 compares the enrollment and number of degrees awarded in 2014 by CSU for the –0.5% decrease in effectiveness ("low") and the 1.5% effectiveness improvement ("high"). In both cases, we held efficiency constant. Note that high efficiency increases the total number of degrees awarded even with reduced enrollment (since students flow through the system faster), whereas low efficiency produces fewer degrees but increases enrollment by "clogging up" the system with students repeating grades.

EFFECTS OF STUDENT FEES AND AID

Higher student fees can increase the revenues available for undergraduate education, but they can also affect potential students'

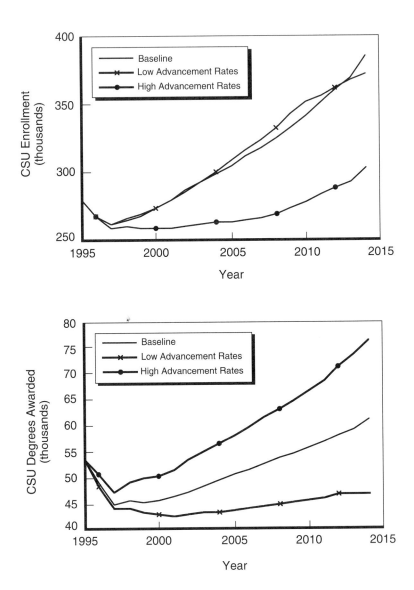

Figure 7—Effect of Alternative Assumptions About Feasible Effectiveness Improvements on CSU Enrollment and Degrees Awarded

decisions on whether to enroll in a public college or university. Thus, fees represent an important decision for policymakers and have been a topic of much debate in recent years.

In our analysis, we estimated the impact of fees on enrollment by varying the participation rates based on data concerning the sensitivity of students to changes in the price of higher education. As discussed in detail in Appendix B, we used data compiled by Kane (1995) of the National Bureau of Economic Research. Using national data, Kane estimated the effects of tuition increases on enrollment in systems within the same state. He found that a $1,000 tuition increase (in 1991 dollars) at public four-year universities decreases enrollment in four-year public institutions by 1.2%, increases enrollment at public two-year colleges by 0.5%, and increases enrollment at private colleges and universities by 0.5%. Kane also found that a $1,000 tuition increase at public two-year colleges decreases enrollment in these colleges by 4.7%, increases enrollment at public four-year universities by 1.8%, and increases enrollment at private colleges and universities by 0.4%. While Kane's data are among the best available, they are hardly definitive. Thus, we considered alternative estimates of the sensitivity of student demand to changes in tuition, ranging from no sensitivity to a sensitivity three times that measured by Kane (see Table 4).

In our analysis, we treated potential fee increases differently than we did the other parameters. We regard fees as a policy lever that can be influenced by the California Education Round Table, whereas we regard the other parameters as exogenous factors largely outside the Round Table's control. Rather than examine the implications for access and our other measures for a range of potential fee increases, we examined (see Chapter 3) what fee increases are necessary to preserve access as a function of the other uncertainties. To help defray the cost of a higher education, many students receive financial assistance from a variety of sources, including federal and state grants and loans, as well as grants and loans from the institutions they attend. For our purposes, we assumed that state and federal aid remains constant as fees change, but that each institution recycles part of the revenues it receives from fee increases into its need-based institutional aid programs. Thus, our fee increases represent the net,

Table 4

Estimates of Price Elasticity and Future Fee Increases

Estimate	Description	Result in 2014
Price elasticity	The constant K in Eq. B3 is a scaling factor for elasticities estimated by Kane (1995) and ranges from 0 to 3.	With K=3 (3 times Kane's estimates), a 3% annual increase in UC and CSU fees would reduce enrollment (and thus decrease access) by about 10%.
Fees	Fee increases reduce admissions of first-time freshmen as described by Eq. B2.	With a 7% annual increase, net fees would increase 360% over 1995 levels. Students at UC, CSU, and the CCs would pay on average $13,500, $6,500, and $700 in fees, respectively.

average increase in the price of education seen by students after receiving financial aid. As a comparison to the fee increases we consider in Chapter 3, note that a report issued by the California Higher Education Policy Center (Callan, et al., 1996) recommends that (1) fee increases not exceed 6%, 5%, and 4% per year at UC, CSU, and the CCs, respectively; and (2) the state provide student financial aid equal to one-third of student fee increases. Many also advocate that fees should rise no faster than the rate of inflation.

Figure 8 shows the effects of a 3% annual fee increase on UC enrollment for a scenario comprising optimistic funding from the state and low efficiency improvements, and using Kane's data for the sensitivity of enrollments to tuition (K=1 in Eq. B3). Note that while fee hikes increase the revenues per student for the systems (allowing more students), they simultaneously price out students through price elasticity (reducing enrollment). Thus, fee increases help preserve access only to the extent that the revenue increase compensates for the fact that increased prices tend to reduce the number of students willing or able to enroll.

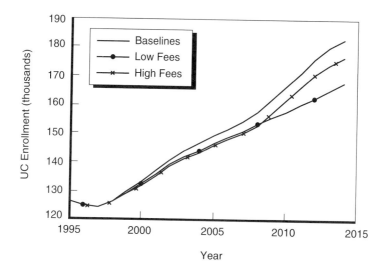

Figure 8—Effect of Student Fees on UC Enrollment

Chapter Three

LANDSCAPES OF PLAUSIBLE FUTURES

So far we have discussed the implications of trends, assumptions, and levers, considered one at a time. This chapter discusses the "landscapes of plausible futures" that we created to show how the interaction of these factors will affect the future of California higher education.

FUNDING AND PRODUCTIVITY TRENDS ARE KEY

A key conclusion of our study is that California's ability to provide widespread access to a college education over the next 15 years is dominated by three key questions: How much funding will the state provide for higher education? How feasible are significant improvements in productivity? Can a high-fee/high-aid system of public education preserve access for California's diverse population? We present the first part of our argument here, showing that any future access deficits depend strongly on what happens to allocations from the state general fund and on the level of improvements in efficiency. For simplicity, we focus on UC first, then broaden the discussion to include CSU and the CCs.

Figure 9 shows the UC access deficit in 2014 for 25 scenarios, each with its own set of assumptions about future levels of state funding for higher education in California and about feasible improvements in efficiency, the first of the two types of productivity improvements we considered. This figure represents each scenario with a colored box that shows the degree of access deficit in 2014 for a particular pair of assumptions about funding and efficiency improvements.

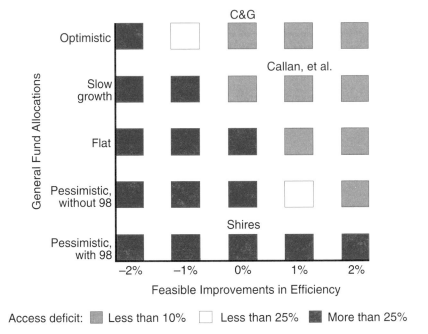

Figure 9—UC Access Deficits in 2014 for 25 Scenarios with Different
Assumptions About State Funding and Feasible
Efficiency Improvements

What is shown is a summarization of many line graphs of the type
presented in Chapter 2. For instance, the boxes labeled "C&G" and
"Shires" in Figure 9 correspond, respectively, to the "optimistic" and
"pessimistic" lines in Figure 4.

It is clear from Figure 9 that UC cannot maintain current levels of access through 2014 if allocations from the state general fund decrease
or if efficiency improvements do not offset cost increases for the inputs to higher education (i.e., if efficiency does not increase by 1% or
2% annually). With the pessimistic allocation of state funds, UC can
maintain its performance only with very large increases in efficiency,
and then only if the allocation of state funds is not subject to
Proposition 98 constraints. With Proposition 98 constraints, UC can
make up the funding shortfall in none of our scenarios. On the other
hand, if efficiency improvements are insufficient for offsetting cost

increases for the inputs to higher education, even the most optimistic general fund scenarios cannot prevent an access deficit and maintain current levels of degree production at UC.

It is useful to compare our results with projections made by others looking at the future of California higher education: (1) Shires (1996) of the California Policy Institute, (2) Cooperud and Geiser (1996) of the UC Research and Planning Department, and (3) Callan, et al. (1996) of the California Higher Education Policy Center. We use these comparisons to make two important points. First, the comparisons help validate our model of the California higher education system. Since we can reproduce the results of these other studies, our model must be reasonably consistent with those currently in use. Second, we show that these different projections are not primarily caused by differences in data and analytic methodology. Rather, the different projections embody fundamentally different assumptions about the future. It is not currently possible (nor may it ever be possible) to resolve these differences with available data and models. Thus, the divergent projections found in today's debate are to be expected and are not likely to be resolved anytime soon.

Shires projects a pessimistic future for California higher education. He assumes that real costs will remain constant with inflation, that state funding for higher education will drop by roughly 1% per year, and that student demand will grow by about 25% over the next 10 years. As shown in Figure 9, the Shires projections correspond to our scenario with "pessimistic, with 98" funding and no change in efficiency. Shires bases his pessimistic assumptions about state funding for higher education on an analysis of future demands on the state budget. He notes that 82% of the state budget currently goes to K–14 education (K–12 plus the CCs), corrections, and health and welfare— all areas that are increasing (and in some cases are mandated by the state constitution or federal government).[1] As shown in Figure 9, our analysis agrees with that of Shires: if these trends continue, they will cause very severe access deficits at UC.

---

[1]In 1996, federal welfare reform legislation replaced federally mandated welfare entitlements with block grants to the states. It is unclear how this change will affect California's overall welfare spending over the next 20 years.

Copperud and Geiser (1996) prepared enrollment estimates based on what they see as the best, worst, and most likely case allocations from the state general fund. The worst-case projections are similar to those of Shires. The most likely case assumes undergraduate enrollments based on 1995 participation rates, productivity improvements that keep up with inflation, and the state adhering to its intent (expressed in the Supplemental Report of the 1994 Budget Act) to increase annual funding to UC and CSU by the marginal cost of educating additional enrolled students. These projections correspond to our scenario with an optimistic general fund allocation and no change in efficiency. As shown in Figure 9, our analysis agrees with the analyses of Copperud and Geiser: these trends, if they continue, will allow UC to avoid serious access deficits.

Callan, et al. (1996) propose a "new compact for shared responsibility" to enhance opportunity in California higher education. They advocate increasing state allocations to higher education as the number of students grows, but argue that productivity improvements can be used to keep this funding from rising as fast as the student population. They suggest a combination of strategies that UC, CSU, and the CCs could use to provide the same or higher levels of educational opportunity while reducing operating costs by about 1% annually. Their projections thus suggest that state funding needs to increase 1.5% annually to accommodate their projected 2.5% annual growth in student population. Overall, their projections correspond to our scenario with slow growth in general fund allocations and 1% annual improvements in efficiency. As shown in Figure 9, our estimates agree with those of Callan, et al.: in this particular scenario, UC avoids serious access deficits.

LEVEL OF DEMAND IS LESS IMPORTANT TO ACCESS

We have argued that access to California higher education in 2014 depends strongly on state funding and feasible levels of efficiency improvements. We now show that access is relatively insensitive to uncertainty about another factor often at the center of recent policy debates—the growing demand for higher education among students. In particular, the results of our analysis suggest that (1) whether or not the precise level of student demand is important depends strongly on trends in state funding and efficiency improvements, and

(2) no plausible assumptions about student demand can save the situation if either funding or efficiency trends are adverse.

Figure 10 shows the UC access deficit in 2014 for 100 scenarios. As in Figure 9, each scenario has a different set of assumptions about future state funding and feasible efficiency improvements, but this time an additional dimension—student demand for higher education—has been added in order to examine the effect of three exogenous trends. As in Figure 9, the lower left-hand corner shows scenarios with low efficiency improvements and pessimistic general fund allocations, and the upper right-hand corner shows scenarios with large efficiency improvements and optimistic general fund allocations. What has been added is how the access deficit varies with the

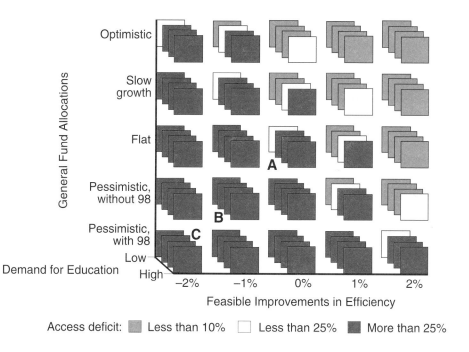

Figure 10—UC Access Deficits in 2014 for 100 Scenarios with Different Assumptions About State Funding, Feasible Efficiency Improvements, and Student Demand

level of student demand, which can be seen by looking at the "stacks" of four boxes within each column. The boxes at the front of the stacks (i.e., the boxes closest to the reader) show scenarios with high student demand; the boxes at the back of the stacks (i.e., those furthest from the reader) show scenarios with low student demand. The boxes second from the back represent the scenarios of Figure 9.

Fourteen of the 25 stacks in Figure 10 are either all red or all green. In these 56 scenarios, the level of student demand makes little difference to the ultimate outcome.[2] Bad situations remain bad and good situations remain good, independent of assumptions about how many students seek admission to UC. However, in four stacks, the access deficit goes from small (green) to large (red) as student demand increases. In these cases, student demand significantly impacts the access deficit.

We assert that the uncertainty in student demand has less impact on access deficit than does the uncertainty in state funding and in potential productivity changes. The reason for this is that demand is constrained by demographics (virtually all the members of the class of 2014 have already been born), whereas (1) state funding of higher education, which has dropped significantly over the past 20 years, will only avoid continuing to drop over the next 15 years if other long-standing trends are broken, and (2) productivity, which has improved significantly over the last decades in numerous sectors of the economy, might also improve in higher education.

EFFECTIVENESS TRENDS ARE IMPORTANT TO MAINTAIN

We also found that access to CSU and the CCs in 2014, like access to UC, depends strongly on assumptions about future state funding and feasible increases in efficiency and is relatively less sensitive to assumptions about student demand. Figure 11 shows the importance of state funding and efficiency improvements for CSU. However, its third dimension differs from the one used in Figure 10. Rather than display the effects of student demand on access deficits, it shows the

---

[2]The level of student demand does change our estimates of the access deficit in these cases, but not by enough for the numeric thresholds represented by the colors to be crossed.

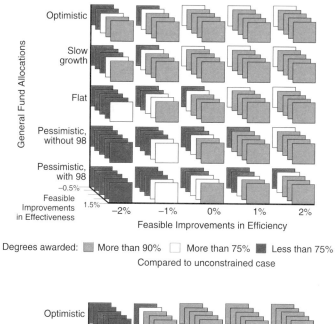

Degrees awarded: ▨ More than 90%   ☐ More than 75%   ■ Less than 75%
Compared to unconstrained case

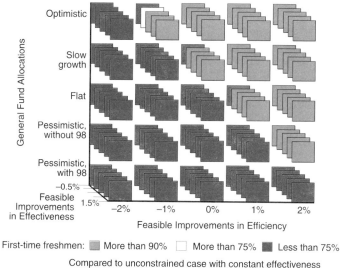

First-time freshmen: ▨ More than 90%   ☐ More than 75%   ■ Less than 75%
Compared to unconstrained case with constant effectiveness

**Figure 11—CSU Bachelor's Degrees Awarded and First-Time Freshmen
in 2014 for 125 Scenarios with Different Assumptions About State
Funding, Feasible Efficiency Improvements, and Feasible
Effectiveness Improvements**

effects of feasible improvements in effectiveness, our second measure of productivity. What it demonstrates is that improvements in effectiveness (1) can significantly affect the number of CSU graduates, but (2) cannot maintain access when trends in funding and efficiency improvements are adverse.

Figure 11 consists of two panels. The upper panel shows the number of degrees awarded in 2014 at CSU for 125 scenarios, each with a different set of assumptions about future allocations of state funding for higher education, feasible improvements in efficiency, and feasible improvements in effectiveness. The lower panel shows the number of first-time freshmen admitted to CSU in 2014 for the same 125 scenarios. One can see how the number of degrees awarded and the number of first-time freshmen vary with improvements in effectiveness by looking at the 25 stacks of boxes in the upper and lower panels, respectively. The boxes at the front of the stacks show scenarios with significant improvements in effectiveness; the boxes at the back show scenarios with annual decreases in effectiveness. The boxes second from the back in the stacks show a scenario with no change in effectiveness, similar to the scenarios we showed in Figure 10.

Figure 11 shows that the number of degrees awarded by CSU in 2014 depends strongly on the level of feasible improvements in effectiveness, as well as on state funding allocations and improvements in efficiency. For instance, CSU cannot maintain its production of degrees, even in the most optimistic funding and efficiency improvement scenarios, if its advancement and graduation rates drop by 0.5% annually, as seen in the upper right-hand corner of the top panel in Figure 11. This suggests that any increases in efficiency cannot come at the expense of the effectiveness of the institution.

Conversely, CSU can maintain its production of degrees in scenarios with flat state funding and no efficiency improvements (0%) if it can increase its advancement and graduation rates by 0.5% to 1.5% annually, as seen in the middle of the top panel.

Effectiveness improvements do not, however, significantly impact access, as measured by the number of first-time freshmen shown in the bottom panel of Figure 11.[3] Twenty-two of the 25 stacks in this panel are all red or green. In these scenarios, effectiveness improvements make little difference to the ultimate outcome. In only three stacks do improvements in effectiveness change the number of freshmen admitted from red to green. Thus, Figure 11 demonstrates that effectiveness improvements can maintain the number of graduates produced by CSU even in scenarios where trends in state funding and efficiency are unfavorable, but that they cannot, by themselves, maintain access when these trends are adverse. We found similar results for UC and the CCs.

DIFFERENCES AMONG SYSTEMS

Until now, we have emphasized the similarities among the UC, CSU, and CC systems because all three respond fundamentally the same way to trends in state funding, productivity, and student demand. Nonetheless, there are important differences, particularly between the CCs and the other two systems. Figure 12 shows the access deficit in 2014 at the CCs for 100 scenarios, each with a different set of assumptions about state funding, efficiency improvements, and student demand. This figure is analogous to Figure 10 for UC.

Figure 12 demonstrates that access to the CCs, like access to UC and CSU, depends strongly on feasible improvements in efficiency. However, access to the CCs depends somewhat less strongly on state funding allocations and more strongly on student demand than does access to UC or CSU. The CCs are more sensitive to demand because they draw from a much larger spectrum of potential students (both part and full time), many of whom technically repeat grades more frequently than their UC and CSU counterparts. Figure 12 shows this enhanced dependence on demand—in eight of the 25 stacks (compared to four in Figure 10), increased demand changes the access deficit from small (green) to large (red).

---

[3]We used first-time freshmen rather than CSU access deficit as our measure of access in Figure 11 because improvements in efficiency actually increase the access deficit. This result stems from the fact that access deficit is a measure of total enrollment, which drops as students move more quickly through the system, as shown in Figure 7. However, as fewer upperclassmen linger in the system, space becomes available to admit more freshmen. These relationships emphasize the importance of looking at several metrics when examining the performance of a complicated system.

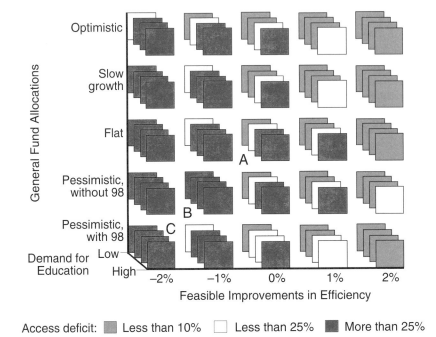

Access deficit: ■ Less than 10%   □ Less than 25%   ■ More than 25%

Figure 12—CC Access Deficits in 2014 for 100 Scenarios with Different Assumptions About State Funding, Feasible Efficiency Improvements, and Student Demand

The CCs are less sensitive than UC and CSU to state general fund allocation because nearly half of their revenue comes from local property taxes. Figure 12 shows this relative insensitivity—in scenarios with no change in efficiency and baseline student demand, the CCs can maintain access deficits smaller than 25% even in the most pessimistic funding scenarios. In contrast, UC and CSU have access deficits greater than 25% in these scenarios. In addition, note that the CCs fare better with the "pessimistic, with 98" funding allocation than with the "pessimistic, without 98" allocation, whereas the two other systems fare significantly better with the latter. This result stems from the fact that Proposition 98 mandates a certain percentage of the state general fund to K–14 education, thus diverting funds to the CCs at the expense of UC and CSU.

LARGE FEE INCREASES MIGHT PRESERVE ACCESS

So far in the 1990s, fees for California public higher education have risen significantly. California retains, however, low tuition and fees compared to other states, and further fee hikes remain a widely discussed policy option for addressing future access deficits. We found that large fee increases, at a rate that would roughly triple current fees by 2014, might preserve California's historic levels of access, but only if the sensitivity of students' enrollment decisions to the price of education is lower than currently estimated (Kane, 1995). If this sensitivity to price is the same as or greater than the current best estimates in the academic literature, fee increases cannot save the situation if funding and efficiency trends are adverse.

Figure 13 shows the annual fee increases needed to preserve access at each of the three systems—UC, CSU, and the CCs—for three different sets of assumptions (labeled A, B, and C in Figures 10 and 12) about future state funding, feasible efficiency improvements, and student demand for education. Set A assumes no growth in state funding, 0% efficiency improvements, and the basecase level of student demand for higher education. Set B assumes pessimistic funding without Proposition 98 constraints, -1% efficiency improvements, and basecase demand; set C assumes pessimistic funding with Proposition 98 constraints, –2% efficiency improvements, and basecase demand. For current fee levels, all three sets of assumptions produce large access deficits for UC, CSU, and the CCs in 2014, as seen also in Figures 10, 11, and 12.

The top panel in Figure 13 shows the fee increases needed to preserve access at UC (i.e., to reduce the access deficit to 10% or less) for each of the three sets of assumptions about funding and efficiency improvement as a function of different assumptions about the sensitivity of student enrollment decisions to price (elasticity). One can see that annual fee increases of less than 2% do not generate enough revenue to preserve access in even the least pessimistic of our three sets of assumptions. Annual increases greater than 2% can relieve access deficits in scenario A (no growth funding, 0% efficiency improvement) as long as elasticity is not too large, but cannot do so in the more adverse scenarios. If elasticity is small—about 30% below that estimated by Kane (1995)—fee increases greater than 5% can

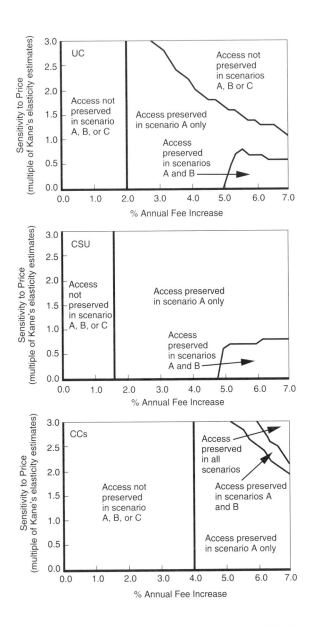

Figure 13—Effect of Fees on UC, CSU, and CC Access Deficits in 2014 as a Function of Student Sensitivity to Price of Education for Three Sets of Assumptions About Future State Funding, Feasible Efficiency Improvements, and Student Demand

also preserve access in scenario B (pessimistic funding without Proposition 98 constraints, –1% efficiency improvement). No level of fee increases that we considered can preserve access in scenario C (pessimistic funding with Proposition 98, –2% efficiency improvement).

Fee increases have a similar effect at CSU, as shown in the middle graph of Figure 13. Increases greater than 2% preserve access in scenario A, increases greater than 5% preserve access in scenario B if elasticity is low, and no increases we considered preserve access in scenario C. In contrast to the UC case, however, large fee increases with large elasticities also preserve access in scenario A, because of the "cascade" effect: many students who choose not to enroll in UC under these conditions enroll in CSU instead.

The results for the CCs, shown in the bottom graph of Figure 13, exhibit an even stronger dependence on this cascade effect. Much larger fee increases are needed to preserve access because fees are a much smaller fraction of the CCs' budgets than they are of the UC and CSU budgets. In addition, high elasticities preserve access to the CCs because more students decide not to enroll in the more expensive UC and CSU systems. It is important to note, however, that although in these high-fee/high-elasticity scenarios the CCs continue to serve over 90% of the total number of students they would under ideal conditions, these high enrollments may be achieved by serving a considerably different student population than the CCs serve today.

With the largest fee increases shown in Figure 13, students in 2014 would pay three times as much as they did in the early 1990s for an education in California's public colleges and universities. Tuition and fees would average $13,500, $6,500, and $700 at UC, CSU, and the CCs, respectively. We assumed that a fraction of the revenues derived from these increased fees would be recycled into need-based institutional financial aid so that actual fees would be higher for wealthier students and lower for poorer ones. The analysis we present in Figure 13 is thus quite crude, because we used a single elasticity for students across a wide range of socioeconomic backgrounds and have not explicitly considered aid separately from fees. Nonetheless, our analysis is sufficient for drawing two conclusions.

First, California would need very large fee increases to maintain current levels of access if allocations from the state general fund decrease or if efficiency improvements do not offset cost increases for the inputs to higher education. The necessary fee increases would push California well into the ranks of high-fee/high-aid public universities by 2014; the CCs would become average-cost institutions compared to similar institutions in other states.

Second, whether California could maintain its historic high levels of access in such a high-fee/high-aid environment is very much an open question, the answer to which depends on factors such as the elasticity of student demand. No one currently knows whether students' sensitivity to price is such that high-fee/high-aid policies could be crafted to preserve access.

Chapter Four

CONCLUSIONS

We have shown through our "landscapes of plausible futures" how the interrelationship of three key factors—demand for higher education, competition for state revenues, and potential productivity improvements—may affect the future of California higher education. We have also shown that the second and third of these factors dominate the question of access. California must maintain the fraction of the state general fund allotted to higher education or make significant productivity improvements in the higher education sector if it is to avoid very large access deficits. Accurate predictions of future demand and decisions about the level of student fees can be important in determining whether there will be access deficits if the system is on the cusp of serious trouble. However, if either productivity or general fund allocations fall toward one of the pessimistic scenarios we reviewed, participation rates will be largely irrelevant to understanding or solving the problem of access. Fee increases tripling the price students now pay for their education might preserve access, but only if students are less sensitive to price increases than currently estimated. California can maintain its current rate of awarding bachelor's degrees in the face of pessimistic funding scenarios if its graduation rates can be increased to levels currently found in other states. However, graduation rate improvements will not address problems of access.

Our study stresses the large uncertainties facing the future of California higher education. In our view, these uncertainties are real and a fundamental part of the problem facing the Round Table and other decision makers concerned with higher education. The landscapes of plausible futures are relatively insensitive to assumptions about the participation rate because uncertainty about the future demand for education is bounded by demographics. All the members of the class of 2014 are alive today, and most are enrolled in California schools. However, California's long-standing financial commitment to higher education is caught in the middle of long-standing, powerful, and conflicting trends. The public resists growth in total government spending at a time when spending on social services and corrections, also driven in part by demographics, continues to grow. Every funding scenario we show in our landscapes, from the most optimistic to the most pessimistic, requires that at least one long-standing trend be broken.

Similarly, over the last few decades, many institutions throughout the U.S. have prospered by changing their organizations and uses of technology so as to achieve significant improvements in their cost structures and the effectiveness with which they perform their missions. Others have not prospered, because they have not made such changes, have made the wrong changes, or have implemented changes poorly. Higher education is clearly different from the profit-making, private sector institutions that provide most of the examples of significant productivity increases. Nonetheless, the present time is fluid enough that the range of productivity increases shown in our landscapes seems a fair representation of the uncertainty as to what improvements may be possible.

Large uncertainty is not a bar to effective decision making. Managers routinely craft flexible, robust strategies that can take advantage of a wide variety of opportunities while avoiding the serious consequences of a wide variety of vicissitudes. However, the first step in crafting such a strategy is to pay sufficient attention to the key uncertainties about the future. The debate over the future of California higher education too often seems to shy away from addressing the central issues. It is not unreasonable to debate small fee increases or fees and projections of future demand; however, doing so makes implicit assumptions about future state funding and productivity improvements.

Overall, the future of California higher education rests on three questions: Can the state readjust its financial commitments in order to maintain current funding levels for higher education? Can the higher education system improve its productivity significantly faster than it has over the past 35 years? and Can high-fee/high-aid public higher education successfully serve a broad spectrum of California's diverse population?

MODELING ENROLLMENT AND DEGREES

This appendix describes the details of the enrollment model used to generate the results given in Chapters 2 and 3. Our model builds on the "participation rate" methodology used by Michael Shires (1996), which is based on the demographics of California's general population. Like Shires, we draw upon this population to model the number of first-time freshmen in UC, CSU, and the CCs broken down into ethnic, age, and gender cohorts. Then, we model the flow of each cohort of admitted students between systems and classes (freshman, sophomore, junior, and senior), as shown in Figure A.1. Unlike Shires, we also consider the effect of students who repeat classes and drop out; we also estimate the number of bachelor's degrees granted from the number of seniors in UC and CSU, including those students who have transferred from the CCs.

CALCULATION OF FRESHMAN ENROLLMENT

We model the number of first-time freshmen (FTF) of a given ethnicity, gender, and age as

$$FTF(system, ethnicity, gender, age, xt, year)$$
$$= Demog(ethnicity, gender, age, year) \qquad \text{(A1)}$$
$$* cPRT(system, ethnicity, gender, age, xt, year)$$

where $Demog(ethnicity, gender, age, year)$ is the projected population in California of a given ethnicity, gender, and age cohort in a given

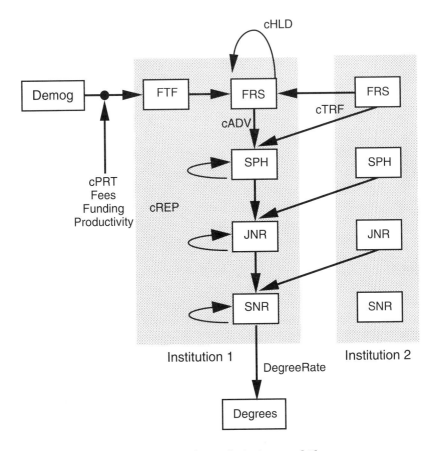

Figure A.1—Student Admissions and Flows

year;[1] the participation rate *cPRT(system,ethnicity,gender,age,xt,* *year)* represents the fraction of each population cohort that becomes freshmen in each system each year; and *xt* indexes full-time vs. part-time status. In the unconstrained admissions case (see Chapter 2), the full number of FTF calculated above is assumed to be admitted into the various systems. In the constrained admissions case,

---

[1]Other groups have used projected high school graduates as the baseline input. Except for factoring an assumed coefficient for high school graduation rate, these two methods should be equivalent.

only a subset of this calculated number is assumed to be admitted. This process is described in detail in Appendix B.

We take *Demog(ethnicity,gender,age,year)* from population projections for each of 100 cohorts[2] provided by the California State Demographic Research Unit (1995). We estimate participation rates from California Postsecondary Education Commission (CPEC, 1995b) data on the number of FTF from 1993 to 1995 in the UC, CSU, and CC systems.[3] We parse these data to generate historical populations of FTF broken down into the cohorts listed above.[4] We then use demographic data for each cohort from 1993 to 1995 to find the average participation rate:

$$cPRT(system,ethnicity,gender,age,xt)$$

$$= \frac{1}{3} \sum_{year=1993}^{1995} \frac{FTF(system,ethnicity,gender,age,xt,year)}{Demog(ethnicity,gender,age,year)} \quad \text{(A2)}$$

Following Shires, we use the value for the FTF (from Eq. A1) to calculate the total number of enrolled freshmen as

$$FRS(sys,year) = FTF(sys,year)$$
$$+ cHLD_1(sys) * FRS(sys,year-1) + TRF_1(sys) \quad \text{(A3)}$$

where $cHLD_1(sys)$ is the percentage of freshmen in each system who repeat their freshman year and $cTRF_1(sys)$ is the number of students from other systems who transfer in as freshmen. We assume these coefficients remain constant over time and estimate them using CPEC data on (1) the enrollment for each system by class, ethnicity, gender, full-/part-time status, and year; (2) the number of transfers

---

[2] In our model, the state's population is broken down into 100 cohorts of ethnicity (Asian, black, Hispanic, white, and other), gender (male and female), and age group (10 categories ranging from 0 to 99+ years old).

[3] Unless otherwise stated, all historical student data for the state were obtained from CPEC data files. Although CPEC has data going further back than 1993, it is sufficient here to average over only the last three years of data.

[4] Actually, the original data have FTF broken into cohorts of ethnicity, gender, full-/part-time status, and year. To assign an age distribution, we used the age distribution of the entire freshman class (which includes transfers and holdovers from previous years, thus slightly skewing the age higher).

between systems by source system, destination system, class, ethnicity, gender, full-/part-time status, and year; and (3) the number of FTF.

CALCULATION OF SOPHOMORE, JUNIOR, AND SENIOR ENROLLMENT

Analogously to what we did for the freshman class, we write the number of students enrolled as sophomores, juniors, and seniors in each system as

$$SPH(sys, year) = cADV_2(sys) * FRS(sys, year-1)$$
$$+ cHLD_2(sys) * SPH(sys, year-1) + cTRF_2(sys)$$

$$JNR(sys, year) = cADV_3(sys) * SPH(sys, year-1)$$
$$+ cHLD_3(sys) * JNR(sys, year-1) + cTRF_3(sys) \qquad \text{(A4)}$$

$$SNR(sys, year) = cADV_4(sys) * JNR(sys, year-1)$$
$$+ cHLD_4(sys) * SNR(sys, year-1) + cTRF_4(sys)$$

where the first term on the right side of each equation is the number of students that advanced into that class from a lower class, the second term is the number that remained in the same class from the previous year, and the third term is the number that transferred into that class from another system. Unfortunately, we cannot calculate the advancement and holdover rate coefficients directly, because the existing data do not distinguish members of a class who advanced from the previous class (e.g., sophomores who were previously freshmen) from members of that class held over from the previous year (e.g., students who repeat their sophomore year)—there are no data on "first-time" sophomores. We can, however, estimate these coefficients indirectly, as described next.

Shires writes the number of enrolled sophomores, juniors, and seniors as

$$SPH(sys, year) = cADV_2{}'(sys) * FRS(sys, year - 1) + cTRF_2(sys)$$
$$JNR(sys, year) = cADV_3{}'(sys) * SPH(sys, year - 1) + cTRF_3(sys) \qquad \text{(A5)}$$
$$SNR(sys, year) = cADV_4{}'(sys) * JNR(sys, year - 1) + cTRF_4(sys)$$

Shires estimates his effective advancement rates, $cADV'(sys)$, for years with available data, as the ratio between two adjacent classes. Using this general method, we find, for instance,

$$cADV_2{}'(sys) = \frac{1}{3} \sum_{year=1993}^{1995} \frac{SPH(sys, year) - cTRF_2(sys)}{FRS(sys, year - 1)} \qquad \text{(A6)}$$

where the summation is used to average over three years. Similar ratios give $cADV_3{}'(sys)$ and $cADV_4{}'(sys)$. Historically, these ratios are relatively stable over time.

We can now combine Eqs. A4 and A5 to relate $cADV'$ to $cADV$ and $cHLD$. The equations for the sophomore class give

$$cADV_2(sys) * FRS(sys, year - 1) + cHLD_2(sys) * SPH(sys, year - 1)$$
$$= cADV_2{}'(sys) * FRS(sys, year - 1) \qquad \text{(A7)}$$

and similarly for the junior and senior classes.

We can get a second equation for $cADV_n(sys)$ and $cHLD_n(sys)$ by noting that in any given cohort of any given class, the students must either (1) remain in the same class, (2) advance to the next class, or (3) drop out or transfer to another system. Thus

$$cADV_n(sys) + cHLD_n(sys) + cDRP_n(sys) = 1 \qquad \text{(A8)}$$

where $cDRP_n(sys)$ refers to students leaving by dropping out or transferring.

We can now solve for $cADV_n(sys)$ and $cHLDn(sys)$ using Eqs. A7 and A8. We can use dropout and transfer-out data for the UC and CSU systems available in the form of life-tables that track cohorts of students on a year-by-year basis (rather than grade by grade). While these data are not necessarily equivalent in character to the enrollment data (which track students by grades), the fact that we are primarily focusing on those students who stay within the systems rather than those who leave makes this analysis fairly insensitive to the details of the dropout rate. Not surprisingly, the enrollment predictions obtained using this method agree fairly closely with the results obtained by Shires.

For the CCs, we calculate enrollments using Shires's Eqs. A5 because the data available to reliably calculate the coefficients for Eqs. A4 are insufficient. Furthermore, we set the advancement and transfer rates for the junior and senior classes to zero since these classes do not exist in the CCs. We treat transfers from the CCs to the freshman, sophomore, and junior classes at UC and CSU in the same way we treat transfers between the four-year systems. However, we assume CC transfers going into the UC and CSU senior class come from the CC sophomore class, rather than from a nonexistent junior class. Transfers from the CCs are treated as a distinct cohort as they progress through the UC and CSU systems.

CALCULATION OF DEGREES AWARDED

We calculate the number of bachelor's degrees awarded each year by UC and CSU as

$$Degrees(sys, year) = cGRAD(sys) * SNR(sys, year - 1) \tag{A9}$$

where $cGRAD(sys)$ is the graduation rate for each system, broken down into the various student cohorts enumerated above. We use 1993 to 1995 data for the ratios of the number of degrees awarded to the number of seniors in order to calculate $cGRAD(sys)$.[5] The available data also specify the number of degrees awarded to students who transferred from the CCs.[6] Because we track those transfer students separately, we can also project the number of bachelor's degrees awarded to CC students who eventually transfer into UC or CSU.

---

[5] These data may be obtained at the CPEC Website.

[6] From 1993 to 1995, nearly a quarter of all degrees awarded by UC went to such transfers, with nearly one half for CSU.

DETAILS ON ADMISSION CRITERIA AND FEES

CONSTRAINED ADMISSIONS

Appendix A specifies the details of the enrollment model for the case of simple, unconstrained admissions, using Eqs. A4 for UC and CSU and Eqs. A5 for the CCs. For the case of constrained admissions, we assume that the constrained system limits its admissions each year such that the revenues per student remain greater than or equal to the 1995 values. Thus, we write this constraint as

$$Enrollment(sys, year) \leq Enrollment(sys, 1995) * \frac{Revenues(sys, year)}{Revenues(sys, 1995)}$$

(B1)

where *Revenues(sys,year)* are the revenues for undergraduate education in each system estimated as described in Appendix C. We assume that a system admits the maximum number of students each year such that total enrollment satisfies Eq. B1. If revenues are sufficiently large, the system can admit all the students who wish to become FTF, as in Eq. A1. If revenues are insufficient, Eq. B1 becomes the binding constraint and we calculate the number of FTF admitted iteratively, because revenues are a function of the number of fee-paying students enrolled.

In any given scenario, we can set the admissions criteria, constrained or unconstrained, individually for each system. Because of transfers, admissions criteria at one system will affect enrollment at another. Figure B.1 compares enrollment at CSU and revenues per under-

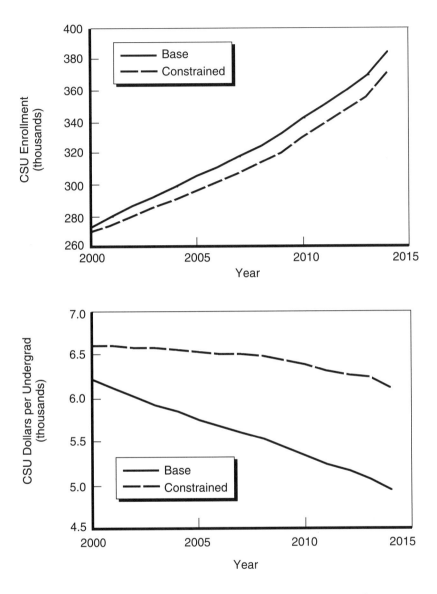

Figure B.1—Effect of Constrained and Unconstrained ("Base") Admissions on CSU Enrollment and Revenues Per Student

graduate in the cases of constrained and unconstrained admissions for the slow-growth scenario for state general fund revenues for higher education. Note that unconstrained (or "base") admissions result in larger enrollments than do constrained admissions, but lead to lower available revenues per student.[1] With unconstrained admissions, alternative assumptions about the allocation of state general funds to higher education have no effect on enrollment, though they can have a large impact on revenues per student. For constrained admissions, increased state funding increases enrollment by raising the number of dollars available for undergraduate education.

EFFECT OF STUDENT FEE CHANGES

In addition to being modified by financial constraints, admissions of FTF can also be modified by changes in student fees. As shown in Chapter 2, Figure 8, changes in student fees can affect potential students' decisions as to whether to enroll in the UC, CSU, and CC systems. We calculate the admission of FTF in each system as a function of the fees by rewriting Eq. A1 as

$$FTF(sys, ethnicity, gender, age, xt, year) =$$
$$Demog(ethnicity, gender, age, year)$$
$$* cPRT(sys, ethnicity, gender, age, xt, year) * ePRC(sys, fees) \quad (B2)$$

where $ePRC(sys, fees)$ is the elasticity of demand for a given system based on the fees in all systems (to allow for both self- and cross-elasticities).

We estimate these elasticities from data compiled by Kane (1995) of the National Bureau of Economic Research. Kane estimates the effects of tuition increases on enrollment in systems within the same state (based on national data). His preliminary findings indicate that

- The effect of a $1,000 (in 1991 $) increase in public two-year tuition is:

---

[1] The apparent decrease in revenues per student in the constrained case arises from the fact that the modeled revenues per student increase from 1995 to 2000; the subsequent decline merely returns this value to the 1995 level by 2014.

> A 4.7% decrease in public two-year enrollment
>
> A 1.8% increase in public four-year enrollment
>
> A 0.4% increase in private enrollment

- The effect of a $1,000 (in 1991 $) increase in public four-year tuition is:

> A 0.5% increase in public two-year enrollment
>
> A 1.2% decrease in public four-year enrollment
>
> A 0.5% increase in private enrollment

In our model, we write these relationships as

$$ePRC\left(sys1, UCfees, CSUfees, CCCfees\right) = \qquad \text{(B3)}$$
$$\prod_{sys2}\left[1 + K \cdot cELS\left(sys1, sys2\right) \cdot \Delta\left(sys2\right)/1000\right]$$

where the product is over the three types of systems, $sys2 = UC, CSU, CC$; $\Delta(sys2) = Fee(sys2, year) - Fee(sys2, year-1)$ gives the year-to-year change in student fees for various systems; K is a simple constant; and $cELS(sys1, sys2)$ is Kane's self- or cross-elasticity for demand at system 1 due to fee changes at system 2. For instance, the effect on CC enrollment of a $1,000 increase in CC tuition is $cELS(CC, CC) = 0.047$. There is little agreement about the value of price elasticities within the education community; values ranging from –0.74 to +0.41 have been cited (Leslie and Brinkman, 1987). We thus consider three alternative values for the constant K: 0, 1, and 3.

DETAILS ON REVENUES ALLOCATED TO EDUCATION

Chapter 2 considered the impact of state general fund revenues as allocations to the UC, CSU, and CC systems. This appendix considers system revenues in more detail.

We write the revenues available for undergraduate education in each of California's three public systems of higher education as the sum of funds given directly to each system from the state and local government, as well as the funds given to each system by each attending student in the form of fees. Thus,

$$
\begin{aligned}
Revenues\ (sys, year) = {}& State(sys, year) + Local\ (sys, year) \\
& + Fee(sys, year) * Enroll\ (sys, year)
\end{aligned}
\tag{C1}
$$

The state funds include contributions from the general fund, lottery revenues, and other state sources. The local revenues, only applicable for the CCs, come from property taxes. In our study, we assumed that these state and local contributions are independent of the number of students attending each system, but that the revenue each system gains from fees is proportional to the number of students enrolled. Our "fees" term includes fees paid directly by the student as well as any financial aid that flows to the system via its enrolled students. Our analysis focuses only on revenues associated with the costs of current operations. We leave the important topic of capital costs for future work.

The state and local funding for each system each year is written as

$$State(sys, year) = State(sys, 1995) * \left[1 + GrowState(sys)\right]^{Year-1995}$$

$$(C2)$$

$$Local(year) = Local(1995) * \left[1 + GrowLocal\right]^{Year-1995}$$

where *State(sys,*1995) and *Local*(1995) are the state and local contributions in 1995, and *GrowState(sys)* and *GrowLocal* are the growth rates describing how the funding changes over time. All three systems get state funding; only the CCs have support from local property taxes. In 1995, UC spent an average of $6,809 in state funds for each of the 153,571 full-time equivalent (FTE) students enrolled. We thus take *State*(UC,1995) = $1,045,665,000. Similarly, CSU spent an average of $4,734 in state funds to educate each of its 252,000 FTE students, so *State*(CSU,1995) = $1,192,968,000. In 1995, the CCs spent an average of $3,050 of state and local funds to educate 858,606 FTE students, with about half of these funds from property taxes, so *State*(CC,1995) = $1,434,681,000 and *Local*(1995) = $1,184,067,000. Dividing California Higher Education Commission values for total revenues from fees by total FTE enrollments in each system gives values for average fees per student as *Fee*(UC,1995) = $3,800, *Fee*(CSU,1995) = $1,850, and Fee(CC,1995) = $200.

DETAILS ON PRODUCTIVITY

In this appendix, we consider in further detail how productivity measures are used and manipulated in our model. In one definition, Epstein (1992) defines productivity improvement as a measurable reduction in cost while maintaining or improving key measures of effectiveness. To address this measure in our simulations, we take the graduation and advancement rates for each system in Eqs. A4 and A9 as our key measures of effectiveness. We define an annual rate of productivity improvement p_1 as the rate at which the minimum revenues needed per student can decrease while the graduation and advancement rates remain unaffected. We thus rewrite Eq. B1 for the maximum enrollment for each system in the constrained admissions case as

$$
\begin{aligned}
Enrollment(sys, year) \leq & \left(\frac{1+\Delta(HEPI)+p_1}{1+\Delta(HEPI)}\right)^{Year-1995} * \\
& Enrollment(sys,1995) * \frac{Revenues(sys, year)}{Revenues(sys,1995)}
\end{aligned}
\tag{D1}
$$

where $\Delta(HEPI)$ is the annual change in the Higher Education Price Index (HEPI), as shown in Figure 6 (see Chapter 2). Note that we have defined the productivity p_1 relative to $\Delta(HEPI)$, so a productivity improvement of $p_1 = 0$ means that the number of dollars necessary for each system to educate an undergraduate just keeps pace with inflation.[1]

Figure 5 (see Chapter 2) compares UC and CSU enrollments for $p_1 = -2\%$ ("low efficiency"), $p_1 = 0\%$ ("flat efficiency"), and $p_1 = 2\%$ ("high efficiency") in the constrained admissions case, assuming the "optimistic" scenario for state general fund revenues. For comparison, enrollments under the unconstrained ("base") admissions case are also presented in the figure. We see that a high rate of productivity growth reduces the access deficit almost to zero, whereas a negative rate of growth causes very large access deficits, similar to the situation for the "pessimistic" estimate of revenues from the state general fund.

In a second definition, Epstein defines productivity improvement as a measurable improvement in some key measure of effectiveness while maintaining or reducing costs. To address this measure, our simulations use either unconstrained admissions or constrained admissions with $p_1 = 0\%$, and define an annual rate of productivity improvement p_2 as the rate at which advancement and graduation rates increase, applied to all the cohorts.[2] Thus,

$$
\begin{aligned}
cAVD_n(sys, year) &= cADV_n(sys) * \left[1 + p_2\right]^{Year-1995} \\
cGRD_n(sys, year) &= cGRD_n(sys) * \left[1 + p_2\right]^{Year-1995}
\end{aligned}
\tag{D2}
$$

Figure 7 (see Chapter 2) shows the effect of variations in the advancement and graduation rates on enrollments and degrees awarded by CSU. Similar results were seen for UC, though the differences between low and high efficiencies were not as great (advancement and graduation rates are higher for UC, so there is less room for improvement).

---

[1] In fact, this method relies on average costs. A similar method can be used to perform this analysis with marginal costs, with some fixed (not proportional to student body) amount of revenues subtracted from the total.

[2] However, values for cADV and cGRD are capped with a maximum value of 1.0. These rates are applied to CC students mainly in terms of the progress of CC transfers through the other two systems.

CALCULATING THE ACCESS DEFICIT

In this appendix, we use the equations laid out in the previous appendices to calculate the access deficit in any given scenario. We write the access deficit as

$$AccessDeficit\left(sys, year, fees\right) = Unconstrained\_Enrollment(sys, year)$$
$$- Constrained\_Enrollment(sys, year, fees)$$

(E1)

Here, the unconstrained enrollments are given by

$$Unconstrained\_Enrollment(sys, year) =$$
$$FTF(sys, year) + cHLD_1(sys) * FRS(sys, year - 1) + TRF_1(sys)$$
$$+ SPH(sys, year) + JNR(sys, year) + SNR(sys, year)$$

(E2)

where we calculate the number of FTF, *FTF(sys,year)*, as the sum over all the ethnic, gender, and age cohorts in Eq. A1 using the participation rate specified for the particular scenario of interest (see Chapter 2's Table 1). The other terms in Eq. E2 are calculated as discussed in Appendix A.

The constrained enrollments are given by

$Constrained \_ Enrollment(sys, year, fee) =$
$$FTF(sys, year, fee) + cHLD_1(sys) * FRS(sys, year - 1) + TRF_1(sys)$$
$$+ SPH(sys, year) + JNR(sys, year) + SNR(sys, year)$$

$$(E3)$$

where the number of FTF, *FTF(sys,year,fee)*, calculated using the participation rate, state funding, and efficiency improvement estimates specified for the particular scenario, is given by the smaller of (1) the sum over all the ethnic, gender, and age cohorts in Eq. B2 or (2) the largest value of *FTF(sys,year,fee)* that satisfies Eq. D1. Note that the *FRS(sys,year)*, *SPH(sys,year)*, *JNR(sys,year)*, and *SNR(sys,year)* terms depend on the *FTF(sys,year,fee)* term in earlier years, so that in general all the terms in Eqs. E2 and E3 will differ each year for any given scenario.

REFERENCES

Bankes, S. C.: 1993, "Exploratory Modeling for Policy Analysis," *Operations Research*, vol. 41, no. 3, 435–449 (also published as RAND RP-211).

Bankes, S. C.: 1994, "Computational Experiments and Exploratory Modeling," *Chance*, vol. 7, no. 1, 50–57 (also published as RAND RP-273).

California State Demographic Research Unit: 1995, *California Public Postsecondary Enrollment Projections, 1995 Series*, 915 L Street, Sacramento, CA 95814.

Callan, Patrick, et al.: 1996, *Shared Responsibility: Strategies to Enhance Quality and Opportunity in California Higher Education*, California Higher Education Policy Center, San Jose, CA.

Carroll, S., E. Bryton, C. P. Rydell, and M. A. Shires: 1995, *Projecting California's Fiscal Future*, MR-570-LE, RAND, Santa Monica, CA.

Copperud, C., and S. Geiser: 1996, *Enrollment Monitoring 1996*, Planning Group Academic Affairs, University of California, Office of the President.

CPEC (California Postsecondary Education Commission): 1995a, *Fiscal Profiles*.

CPEC: 1995b, *California Public College and University Enrollment Demand, 1994 to 2005*, July.

Dewar, J. A., C. H. Builder, W. M. Hix, and M. H. Levin: 1993, *Assumption-Based Planning: A Planning Tool for Very Uncertain Times*, MR-114-A, RAND, Santa Monica, CA.

Epstein, Paul: 1992, "Measuring the Performance of Public Services," in Holzer, Marc (ed.), *Public Productivity Handbook*, Marcel Dekker, Inc., New York.

Kane, Thomas: 1995, "Rising Public College Tuition and College Entry: How Well Do Public Subsidies Promote Access to College?" National Bureau of Economic Research Working Paper 5164, July.

Lempert, Robert J., Michael E. Schlesinger, and Steve Bankes: 1996, "When We Don't Know the Costs or the Benefits: Adaptive Strategies for Abating Climate Change," *Climatic Change*, vol. 33, 235–274.

Leslie, Larry L., and Paul T. Brinkman: 1987, "Student Price Response in Higher Education: The Student Demand Studies," *J. Higher Education*, vol. 58, no. 2, March/April.

Morgan, M. Granger, and Max Henrion: 1990, *Uncertainty: A Guide to Dealing with Uncertainty in Quantitative Risk and Policy Analysis*, Cambridge University Press.

Schwartz, Peter: 1991, *The Art of the Long View*, Doubleday Currency, New York.

Shires, Michael A.: 1996, *The Future of Public Undergraduate Education in California*, MR-561-LE, RAND, Santa Monica, CA.

University of California, Office of the President: 1996, *Enrollment Monitoring 1996*, January.

Wack, P.: 1985, "Scenarios: Shooting the Rapids," *Harvard Business Review*, November–December, 139–150.

Watson, S. R., and D. M. Buede: 1987, *Decision Synthesis: The Principles and Practice of Decision Analysis*, Cambridge University Press, New York.